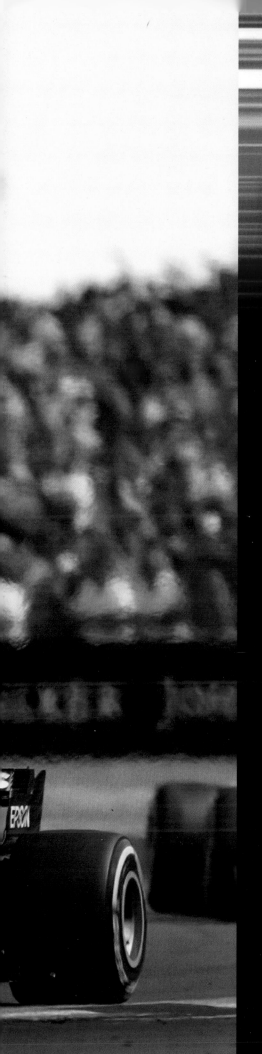

CW00323289

FORMULA ONE 2019

Written by Graham Muncie

Designed by Lucy Boyd

A Pillar Box Red Publication

© 2018. Published by Pillar Box Red Publishing Limited, in association with the Daily Mirror. Printed in the EU.

ISBN 978-1-907823-56-5

CONTENTS

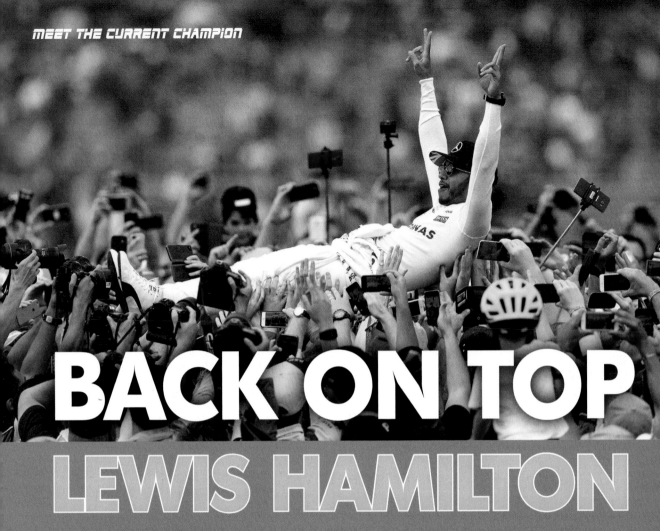

BACK ON TOP
LEWIS HAMILTON

British superstar Lewis Hamilton is widely recognised as one of the All-Time Greats having clinched his fourth World Championship in 2017, becoming one of only five men to ever achieve this level of success.

Although there is work to be done should Hamilton want to reach or eclipse Michael Schumacher and his record seven world titles. At only 33 years old though, time is on Hamilton's side as he goes in chase of the German legend.

Hamilton's title win in 2017 may well go down as his best-ever as he romped to a 46 point margin over Sebastian Vettel, this

being even more remarkable as Vettel had the Championship lead halfway through the season. As he often does, Hamilton went from strength to strength as the season progressed, remarkably winning five out of six races between rounds 12 and 17. This gave the Brit the commanding lead that he would hold on to, clinching the title in Mexico with two races to spare.

Having now won title number four, Hamilton is showing no signs of letting up. He has come a long way since his interest in cars and motor racing started with a gift of a remote controlled car from his father when he was six years old! Immediately, Hamilton started winning Club Championships against adults and, with an obvious natural flair for racing, Hamilton then got his first go-kart at age six. Hamilton was also a talented footballer as a child playing alongside the likes of England international Ashley Young for his school football team and he has often said if things had not worked out as a racing driver he would have pursued a career as a professional footballer, although it is fair to say his talents in motorsport far outstripped his footballing ambitions.

FACTFILE

DATE OF BIRTH:
7th January 1985

BORN: Stevenage, England

BEST EVER CHAMPIONSHIP FINISH:
World Champion 2008, 2014, 2015, 2017

CURRENT TEAM:
Mercedes

Hamilton followed the conventional path to Formula 1 starting at eight years old in karting competitions before moving onto single seater racing and being snapped up by the McLaren driver training programme. Such was the confidence Hamilton had in his abilities that upon meeting former boss Ron Dennis, a 10 year old Hamilton declared that he would be a F1 World Champion one day.

Making his debut in Formula 1 in 2007, the Stevenage-born racer finished in second place in his debut season heartbreakingly missing out on the title by only one point, while setting numerous records for being the youngest driver along the way. This would only deny the Brit his maiden title by a short while though as he duly notched his first title a year later.

The next few years were not so kind as Hamilton's McLaren car became less and less competitive as the years passed, causing Hamilton to seek a move away and join the Mercedes team in 2013. Under the introduction of new car guidelines, Mercedes were set for a big jump and Hamilton joined them to begin his dominant run which began with a fourth place finish before back-to-back World titles in 2014 and 2015, a second placed in 2016, followed by that fourth title in 2017.

Outside of racing, Hamilton is involved in numerous charities and has been awarded an MBE by the Queen for his services to motorsports. Hamilton is also taking on an increased role as an influencer speaking on such topics as race relations, veganism and his charity work, however none of this appears to be taking away any focus on his ultimate drive to be known as the best F1 driver there ever was.

FACE IN THE CROWD

Lewis Hamilton greets the crowds after the 2018 Grand Prix at Silverstone. Can you spot his fellow drivers Vettel, Räikkönen and Bottas?

VETTEL ON THE HUNT
SEBASTIAN VETTEL

After a lean few years, there are signs that German driver, Sebastian Vettel, is getting closer to clinching a fifth world title, a feat that would make him only the third person to ever do so.

Times have been tough for Vettel since his four world title wins in consecutive years between 2010 and 2013, however with his Ferrari car becoming more and more competitive, it seems with every passing Grand Prix there are many predicting that it may not be long until he is atop the podium once more. With a host of F1 records to his name Vettel is currently the most successful driver lining up in F1, although Lewis Hamilton can lay claim to the same number of world titles after his 2017 win.

An interesting character, Vettel has often said that as a youngster, it was not racing drivers but singer, Michael Jackson, that he most wanted to be like. However these hopes were dashed due by Vettel's own admission of 'a lack of talent'. Luckily for the German, what he lacked in singing skills he more than made up for in driving skills and this has taken him to multiple F1 glories.

Vettel was perhaps always destined for the top as despite no real racing pedigree in his family, both he and brother Fabian competed in the Audi Sport TT Cup. He was around racing from a young age, starting karting at the remarkably young age of three years old. By age 11, he was part of the Red Bull Junior Team and accolades were to come at all levels he raced in before making the jump to F1 in 2006 with the BMW Sauber team, originally as third driver and test driver. An injury to BMW regular, Robert Kubica, opened the door for Vettel to make his debut at the USA Grand Prix where he finished eighth becoming at the time the youngest-ever points scorer in a Grand Prix.

This performance earned Vettel a move to Toro Rosso to see out the 2007 season before a full time drive in 2008 and his first ever F1 Grand Prix win. This would come at the 2008 Italian Grand Prix, again being the youngest-ever to achieve this - at the time, Vettel was only 21 years and 74 days

FACTFILE

DATE OF BIRTH:
3rd July 1987

BORN: Heppenheim, Germany

BEST CHAMPIONSHIP FINISH: World Champion 2010, 2011, 2012, 2013

CURRENT TEAM: Ferrari

old. Alongside other notable drives, this win earned him the F1 Rookie of the Year award for best newcomer to the series.

As Toro Rosso is a feeder team for the main Red Bull racing outfit, a promotion was surely on the cards and this duly took place before the 2009 season with Vettel replacing the retired David Coulthard. Things would only get better and better for

Vettel as he finished second in the Championship, a precursor of what was to come as Vettel and Red Bull would then go on to dominate the sport with four consecutive World Championships between 2010 and 2013, Vettel still holding the records of being the Youngest-Ever Champion, scoring the Most Points in a Season and recording the Most Pole Positions in a Season.

However, by 2014 cracks were starting to appear between Vettel and Red Bull with the car's reliability issues causing Vettel to drop down the grid. A disappointing

Championship with a fifth place finish and no race wins confirmed his departure from the team, with Ferrari snapping up his signature.

The following few years with Ferrari were no easier as the famous Italian team struggled for speed, but now four years into his Ferrari experiment, the signs are there that they are back at the top of the grid and, with Vettel determined to claim more glory, no one would be surprised should the German clinch a fifth world title and go in chase of his compatriot and friend, Michael Schumacher's, record of seven titles.

IN IT TO WIN IT

All fans of Formula 1 love the sport for the famous thrills, glamour and speed, not to mention the death-defying overtaking manoeuvres carried out.

But, there are some who do not share our passion (unbelievable right!) saying that F1 is predictable, that it is the same winners all the time and whoever leads into the first corner normally wins the race. Is that really the case though?

A quick look back to the 2017 season shows that this most definitely is not the case, with five different race winners across the season showing just how hard it is to predict the winner of any given Grand Prix. Add to this the fact that eight different drivers recorded the fastest lap of a race and it becomes very easy to dispel the notion that F1 is all about getting to the first corner in front and that it is the same drivers who do this all the time.

Of course there will be spells where one team or driver rules the sport for a few years; just look at Ferrari and Michael Schumacher's domination in the early 2000s or Sebastian Vettel winning a run of four straight title wins all in recent memory, but this could be said of absolutely any sport!

Championships have been won and lost on the final laps of the season and we will now look at the details of some of these passes that have left fans in awe of the ability of the drivers and cars on show.

Mark Webber on Fernando Alonso
Belgian Grand Prix 2012

One of the most feared corners on any F1 circuit is the 'Eau Rouge' at Spa-Francorchamps, the home of the Belgian Grand Prix. Not many even attempt a passing move there, with the vast majority of those that do falling foul of the famous left-right uphill turns that challenges the drivers to just stay on the track let alone pass an opponent.

In 2012, Red Bull driver of the time, Mark Webber, did just that though, taking the kinks flat out, diving past Fernando Alonso just centimetres from the Spaniard's wheels on one side and with two of his own wheels on the kerb on the other. It looked for all to see that Webber would spin out, potentially taking Alonso with him in what would have been a high speed crash, but the Australian made the move hold firm, blasting past Alonso in breathtaking style.

Nigel Mansell on Nelson Piquet
British Grand Prix 1987

One of the biggest rivalries the sport has ever seen was between Britain's Nigel Mansell and Brazilian Nelson Piquet. Despite racing for the same team the two were bitter rivals, each accusing the other of costing them the World Championship, not to mention a spat that almost resulted in legal action being taken by Mansell against Piquet.

The pinnacle of this track rivalry was to come at Silverstone in 1987. Piquet had led the race throughout with Mansell in hot pursuit appearing to stalk his prey and it only being a matter of time before the future World Champion would complete an overtake. When he did though, it was a thing of beauty as he jinked as if to go around the outside of Piquet heading for the famous 'Stowe' corner; at the last moment Mansell cut back under his rival on the inside to take the lead and, with only two laps remaining, it was enough to see Mansell take the chequered flag, with a track invasion from the British fans following.

Mika Häkkinen on Michael Schumacher
Belgian Grand Prix 2000

Another famous pass on the Spa circuit came back in 2000 when then two-time defending World Champion Mika Häkkinen and Michael Schumacher locked horns. Häkkinen (who was leading the Championship at the time) took pole and looked on course for an easy victory. A spin in wet conditions for the Fin allowed Schumacher to take the lead but Häkkinen would not give up.

With three laps to go, Häkkinen was back on the German's tail and this is when he decided to go for one of the most daring moves the sport has seen. Heading for the 'Eau Rouge', Häkkinen decided the only way to get past his opponent was to take the corner at full speed. Something that was never done, let alone on a still-damp track whilst trying to pass an All-Time Great such as Schumacher. Häkkinen has told the story of how he decided to count to three with his foot firmly planted on the accelerator as he knew by the end of that time he would be right on Schumacher's tail or would have crashed out of the race. The plan worked to perfection, however the job was not done yet. Schumacher still held the lead as they approached the next corner, and with backmarker Ricardo Zonta also blocking the way, it looked as if there was no way past. Hakkinen then made a fell swoop. With Schumacher looking to go outside Zonta, the Fin dived inside both of them and into a lead he would not relinquish in one of the most spectacular moves F1 has ever seen.

Lewis Hamilton on Timo Glock
Brazilian Grand Prix 2008

For a pass to be historical it does not always need to be death defying and, while not the most outstanding overtake technically, the importance of this pass cannot be understated. Running in sixth place as he entered the last lap and knowing that this would mean missing out on the title to Felipe Massa, Hamilton set off after Glock in a race that had been driven in almost monsoon conditions at times. The race had been full of drama throughout with many pit changes and

stoppages. Entering that fateful lap, Glock sat in fourth position, but with thunder still clapping in the sky and rain bouncing off the track, he had the major disadvantage of being on dry weather tyres, meaning a complete lap of grip. With Hamilton on the proper tyres, he set off after Glock passing him on the second-to-last corner of the entire season to clinch his first world title by one point, this acting as a springboard to the career Hamilton has went on to achieve.

Champion, Lewis Hamilton, celebrates another win at the Hungarian Grand Prix, July 2018.

DRIVE
THE GLOBE

There is an old saying in sports: "If you are good enough, you are old enough". Well, it could be said that in Formula 1, this could be changed to "If you are good enough, they will find you," as the sport continues to showcase its global presence through the varying nationalities of the drivers that take to the track in every Grand Prix.

A quick look through the starting grid of the opening race of the 2018 season shows that of the 20 drivers competing, there were a whopping 15 different nationalities represented including, Russia, Canada, Monte Carlo, New Zealand, Finland, Netherlands, and Mexico, as well as the perhaps more widely known driver development spots such as the UK, Germany, France and Spain. Add to this the varied places that host Grand Prix and it is easy to see why F1 is widely regarded as one of the most diverse sports on the planet.

This is not a new phenomenon though. As far back as the inaugural championship in 1950, there were 11 different countries represented for fans from that nation to cheer on. Over the history of the F1 Championship 14 different countries could cheer on a Championship, winner with the UK at the top of the list, with 17 Championships won between 10 different drivers. Germany are second with 12, although this has been dominated by the 11 held between Michael Schumacher and Sebastian Vettel. Brazil and Argentina are next on the list showing once again that the sport spans the globe from Europe all the way to South America and with other places such as Australia, South Africa, the United States and New Zealand all having had at least one man crowned Champion. Over the years, 37 different countries have held a Grand Prix and 21 different countries have had a driver of that nationality win a race.

One notable exception may be Asia, but with Grand Prix currently being held in Bahrain, China, Singapore and Abu Dhabi to stoke interest, plus the finances and technology that countries like India and Japan possess, it may not be long until that is righted and one of those countries can lay claim to a Champion of their own.

Why is it then that so many diverse and different countries are represented in F1? There may be many answers to this including sponsorship attraction, teams wanting home grown drivers and availability of drivers local to the team for testing purposes. The main reason for this diversity though is in the way that drivers are noticed by Formula 1 teams. Almost all the drivers will start in local karting competitions in their own countries, either as a hobby that they realise they have a talent for, or they get their start by being part of a racing family.

If they show they are good enough in these local karting events, they will move onto national and international events before taking the leap into single seater car racing. Again, this may be at a national level before they outstrip their opponents in this and move onto the global support tours that follow F1 around the globe. This means that by the time a F1 team is looking to fill a seat, they have a global pool to choose from, most noticeably from the F2 circuit so the talent is already there regardless of nationality.

Of course there will always be certain countries that have a strong presence on the grid and historically the UK has always been one of them. The UK holds both the records for Most Drivers to Claim the Championship and Most Championship Wins by a Nation, with 10 and 17 wins respectively. Over the years, a large selection of F1 teams have called Britain their home. That is not to say that the UK can lay claim to be the home of F1 exclusively though, and each nation has a passionate group of fans who cheer on their heroes wherever they go.

Perhaps most famous are the Italian Ferrari fans known as the 'Tifosi' who make the Italian Grand Prix at Monza a sea of red every year, and can also be seen almost anywhere the F1 circus moves on to.

Japanese fans are also renowned worldwide for the passion and colour they show for their favourite drivers, and the roar heard in Brazil when a Brazilian racer takes the chequered flag is almost unmatched.

Perhaps this is the appeal of Formula 1: no matter where you are from, it is very likely that you will have a hero from your own country to cheer for. Are your favourites from your country or do you support drivers from somewhere else?

F1 really can lay claim to being the most global of all sports as the teams and Championship move around the world on a almost weekly basis during the season, inspiring awe from fans everywhere they go, and who knows, maybe igniting a passion in someone that they will be the next or first great driver to come from their country to get to the top of the podium and stand proudly as their flag is raised and national anthem played!

Sebastian Vettel on track at the Hungarian Grand Prix, July 2018.

VALTTERI BOTTAS

Continuing the history of top level Finnish Formula 1 stars is Mercedes man, Valtteri Bottas. Born in Nastola in Southern Finland, Bottas' rise to the top is a surprising one being that there is little racing pedigree in his family. However, Bottas has been F1 made for as long as he can remember, this being proven by the fact his childhood dog was named after famous F1 driver, Rubens Barrichello.

The familiar tale of karting prodigy turned single seater champion was the path for Bottas as he looked to emulate such compatriots as two-time World Champion Mika Häkkinen in bringing back F1 gold to the small Scandinavian nation.

Making the jump to car racing in 2007 with almost immediate success, Bottas was brought to the attention of many including Toto Wolff, the then-Williams director (and now Mercedes chief), Häkkinen himself and Didier Coton who had been Häkkinen's manager when he was at his most successful. Further success as he

moved up the levels meant that by 2010, he was in place as a test driver for Williams under the tutelage of Wolff.

This arrangement continued until the start of the 2013 season when Bottas would gain a permanent slot in the Williams team. The Williams car was not one of the more competitive on the grid, Bottas finding himself 17th in the standings with only four points to his name. A marked improvement in performance was to come in year two though, as Bottas raced to fourth in the Championship with six podium finishes during the year.

Another solid if unspectacular year was to follow in 2015 with a fifth place Championship finish, followed by an eighth place finish in 2016 in what was to be the Fin's last year with Williams. A shock move to Mercedes was to follow after the retirement of then-World Champion Nico Rosberg and Bottas would make the most of this step up in class, taking his first ever career Grand Prix win and finishing third overall behind

FACTFILE

DATE OF BIRTH:
28th August 1989

BORN: Nastola, Finland

BEST CHAMPIONSHIP FINISH: 3rd, 2017

TEAM: Mercedes

teammate, Lewis Hamilton, and Sebastian Vettel and helping Mercedes retain the Constructors' Championship.

It remains to be seen whether Bottas can make the next step in his career and challenge Hamilton and Vettel for superiority, but with the strides made in his career, there are few who think this is not a possibility.

KIMI RÄIKKÖNEN

One of the most interesting characters to be found in F1 comes in the form of Ferrari's Finnish racer, Kimi Räikkönen.

The 2007 World Champion is known as much for his party attitude as his driving prowess but that is not to take away from one of the most naturally gifted drivers the world has ever seen, as not only has Räikkönen tasted glory in F1 but he has also competed at the World Championship level in both rallying and snowmobile racing also.

Nicknamed the 'Iceman' due to his unflappable personality, Räikkönen is somewhat regarded as a bit of a cold character particularly as he does not seem interested in the media, preferring to keep his private life to himself and just wanting to show up and race.

These characteristics have helped him become one of the most successful drivers racing in F1 with

20 race wins to his name entering the 2018 season and, of course, that Championship gold from 2007.

Räikkönen has also had a varied F1 career having started off with Sauber in 2001. At this time, he only had 23 races in single seater racing to his name and as such the owner of the team, Peter Sauber, had to make a special appeal for the Fin to be granted the licence required to race.

This faith was to be repaid almost immediately achieving a points scoring positon in his debut Grand Prix.

Räikkönen's showings in his debut season earned him a move to McLaren where he would spend the next five seasons improving year on year. A big move to Ferrari was to follow with the World Championship coming in his first year there, becoming the only driver ever to win the title in his first year with the famous team.

FACTFILE

DATE OF BIRTH:
17th October 1979

BORN: Espoo, Finland

BEST CHAMPIONSHIP FINISH:
World Champion 2007

TEAM: Ferrari

This is still the best year of Räikkönen's F1 career but back at Ferrari now, and in a fast improving car, there may be one last hurrah before the enigmatic Fin calls time on his F1 career.

THE MONACO GP

Ask any non-F1 fan to name one Grand Prix circuit and it is more than likely the answer will be Monaco. Why is it that the race around the streets of the principality has become such a famous event in the sporting world gathering crowds from all around the globe?

It is easy to see the appeal. With the stunning settings of Monaco and the luxury that goes with it, it could be said there is as much of a competition to have the biggest yacht moored in the marina or to throw the most lavish party! But how did this all come about?

ORIGINS

The history of the Monaco Grand Prix goes all the way back to 1929 when Prince Louis II of Monaco, then the president of the Automobile Club de Monaco, agreed to allow his streets to host the event. The very first race was held on 14th April organised by Antony Noghès and was an invitation-only event. It was won by Frenchman, William Grover-Williams, (a very interesting character who would go on to became a spy in World War II) racing in a Bugatti Type 35B.

Over the following years, the Monaco Grand Prix raised in stature, at this time there was no official F1 Championship so many races were held under the title of 'Grand Prix' to increase importance. Certain races were given the added title of 'National Grand Prix' meaning they were the official race of that country and in 1933 Monaco was given this status; this was verified further when it was selected as one of the founding races for the new European Championship which launched in 1936.

The race was to continue until 1938 when a demand for appearance money from the top competitors led to the race being cancelled. This being followed by the onset of World War II in 1939, with all organised motor racing in Europe being put on hold.

>> THE MOST SUCCESSFUL DRIVER EVER ROUND THE STREET CIRCUIT IS AYRTON SENNA.

FORMULA 1 HISTORY

In 1950, the Formula 1 World Championship as we now know it was introduced with Monaco to be the flagship race in this new championship. All-Time Great and five-time World Champion Juan Manuel Fangio was to take his first-ever Grand Prix win in 1950, propelling him to greatness. The race was run intermittently over the next few years due to various issues but returned in 1955 and has been an ever-present in the F1 calendar ever since.

The most successful driver ever round the street circuit is Ayrton Senna who won the race a remarkable six times in the space of seven years, including five wins in a row between 1989 and 1993.

Two racers have won the race five times, these being Britain's Graham Hill who was dubbed 'The King of Monaco' due to his record of winning the race three years in a row between 1963 and 1965, then a further double in 1968 and 1969. The other five-

time winner is Germany's Michael Schumacher who dominated the race in the mid to late nineties taking the chequered flag in 1994, 1995, 1997, 1999 and 2001.

In recent times, the race has seen multiple winners spread out but German Nico Rosberg did take a hat-trick of victories between 2013 and 2015 to show the liking he had for the track.

McLaren are the most successful of the constructors having had a driver take the victory 15 times in the history of the race; the remarkable bit about this stat is their first victory did not come until 1984 meaning those 15 victories have come in the last 34 years. Ferrari are second with 10 victories and Lotus and Mercedes share third spot with seven apiece.

CIRCUIT

The Monaco circuit has had a few alterations over the years as safety measures have improved but remains largely similar to the track that the original racers took to back in the day. The current layout has a length of 2.074 miles and a race length of 78 laps, meaning the man to cross that finishing line in first place will have completed almost 162 miles by the time he sees the chequered flag.

Due to the narrow course layout and many elevation changes and tight corners, it is viewed as one of the

most demanding tracks despite it also being one of the slowest. It is also the shortest Grand Prix on the calendar with all others needing to adhere to a minimum 190 mile race distance.

The circuit consists of the city streets of two different towns, Monte Carlo and La Condamine, where the famous harbour section lies. With other famous sections including 'The Tunnel' where racers reach the highest speeds on the circuit just millimetres from the barriers, and with the changing from the natural and usually vibrant sunshine outside to the dimmed lighting of the tunnel causing vision problems, this is one of the ultimate tests of a driver's skill and nerve.

The building of the circuit from the normal streets that any car can drive on the rest of the year takes six weeks to complete and a further three weeks after the event to put back to normal.

A lap of the circuit takes you from the starting point and a short sprint up 'Boulevard Albert Ier', then the tight right-hand 'Sainte-Dévote' corner (so named for a church just beyond the barriers there).

Then comes a long uphill stretch leading to the left handed 'Massenet' corner. You then head past the famous casino to 'Casino Square', the highest part of the track. You will then snake down 'Avenue des Beaux Arts' into the 'Mirabeu', before the iconic 'Fairmont Hairpin,' the tightest and slowest corner on any F1 track.

A double right-hander then follows before entry to the aforementioned Tunnel. This causes all sorts of problems for driver and car as not only is there lost visibility, but the car loses around 30% of its downforce due to the aerodynamic properties of the tunnel. Further issues are caused if it is raining as the tyres go from wet to dry ground. Out of the tunnel and you are in the harbour district and the 'Nouvelle Chicane', then a short change to the 'Tabac' right-hander.

Another fast section comes before 'Piscine' and another chicane. Out of that chicane comes the second tightest corner on the circuit, 'La Rascasse', which requires full steering lock from the cars. Then a short straight before the final corner, 'Virage Antony Noghès', named after the organiser of the first ever Monaco Grand Prix. Then across the line to complete the lap.

Do you think you could do that faster than the current record holder, Max Verstappen, who completed the feat in 1 minute 14.26 seconds?!

FAMOUS MONACO INCIDENTS

There have been many famous and infamous incidents over the history of the Monaco Grand Prix, some due to the daring and skill of the drivers, others due to the very nature of the circuit causing events that could not be replicated at any other race in F1.

One of these events took place in 1955 when twice-World Champion Alberto Ascari crashed at high speed on the chicane exiting the tunnel and actually ended up in the sea! Ascari was leading the race when, either distracted by the crowd's reaction to the fact Stirling Moss had just retired or the fact that he had just lapped Cesare Perdisa, he completely missed the chicane, crashing through barriers, hay bales and sandbags and landing in the sea beyond. His Lancia car narrowly missed an iron bollard by about 30cm before hitting the water and immediately sinking deep into the Mediterranean Sea that borders Monaco. Around three seconds passed before Ascari appeared and was immediately hauled onto a boat, remarkably escaping with just a broken nose.

An occurrence rather more infamous than Ascari's was to unfold in qualifying for the 2006 staging of the race. Michael Schumacher, who held the provisional pole position heading in the third and final round of

> **THE BUILDING OF THE CIRCUIT FROM THE NORMAL STREETS THAT ANY CAR CAN DRIVE ON THE REST OF THE YEAR TAKES SIX WEEKS TO COMPLETE AND A FURTHER THREE WEEKS AFTER THE EVENT TO PUT BACK TO NORMAL.**

qualifying, looked set to lose his pole position as both McLaren were lapping faster as the qualifying round entered the final stages. Schumacher was not to be outdone though as on his final attempt, Schumacher allegedly deliberately lost control on the slow and easy Rascasse Corner, nudging his car into the barriers and blocking the track. The resultant yellow flags meant all other drivers on track had to stop and with this being the final 'flying lap' attempt of the McLarens, Schumacher's pole was intact. This was not to work out for the German though as the stewards promptly demoted him to the back of the grid.

Perhaps the strangest and most controversial event in Monaco's history took place in 1984 when Ayrton Senna thought he had the race won as the race was stopped after 32 laps having passed Prost on that lap. Senna celebrated doing a victory lap; little did he know that the result would stand after lap 31 handing the win to Prost.

There have been many other incidents of note over the almost 90 year history of the Monaco Grand Prix but these examples go to show just why it truly is the Jewel in F1's Crown.

PUT YOUR F1 KNOWLEDGE TO THE TEST!

Award yourself one point for a correct answer – some carry a bonus point for difficulty.

1 Which driver has won the most F1 World Championships ever?

2 How many points did Lewis Hamilton win the 2017 World Championship by?

3 How many different drivers won a Grand Prix in 2017?

4 Where is the British GP held?

5 How many British World Champions has there been in F1 history?

6 What nationality is Sauber's Charles Leclerc?

7 Name the different teams that Lewis Hamilton has driven for. [2pts]

8 Who were McLarens' drivers at the start of the 2018 season? [2pts]

9 How many World Championships has Sebastian Vettel won?

10 Where is the Italian Grand Prix held?

11 How many different countries have hosted a Grand Prix?

12 Which Constructor has the most Constructors' Championships in the history of F1?

13 And how many times has that team won the Constructors' Championship? [2pts]

14 Two drivers made their F1 debuts at the start of the 2018 season – can you name them?

15 Which Grand Prix traditionally starts the F1 Season?

16 Four former World Champions had team places at the start of the 2018 season, can you name them?

17 Which country was Toro Rosso driver Brendon Hartley born?

18 How many different teams started the 2018 F1 season?

19 When was the first Monaco Grand Prix held?

20 Two drivers share the record for most wins in a season, can you name them?

21 How many races did they win in those seasons?

22 How many drivers have crashed through the barriers and ended up in the harbour during a Monaco Grand Prix?

23 Can you name them? [2pts]

24 How many of the teams currently competing in F1 are based in the UK?

25 Which nationality is driver Kevin Magnussen?

26 How many races did Lewis Hamilton win on his way to becoming 2017 World Champion?

27 In what years did McLaren's Fernando Alonso win his World Championships?

28 Which city hosted the 2018 Canadian Grand Prix?

29 Who has won the most Monaco Grand Prix?

30 How many times did he win it?

31 2018 season for Force India.

32 How many races did Max Verstappen win in 2017?

33 Which team did Valtteri Bottas make his Formula 1 debut for?

34 Which two teams did Michael Schumacher win World Championships with?

35 Who has started the most Grand Prix in the history of the sport? [2pts]

36 both won the F1 World Championship?

37 Can you name them? [2pts]

38 How many Grand Prix took place in 1950 (the sport's first ever year)? [2pts]

39 Who holds the record for winning the most Grand Prix without ever winning the World Championship?

40 What is the top speed ever recorded in a F1 car in official competition and who recorded it? [2pts]

HOW DID YOU DO?

40-48 POINTS
World
Champion

30-40 POINTS
Podium
Finish

20-30 POINTS
In the Points
Positions

10-20 POINTS
Developing
Driver

0-10 POINTS
Back to
Go Karting for you!

ANSWERS ON
**PAGE
60-61**

WHY GREAT BRITAIN IS THE HOME OF
»FORMULA 1

Formula 1 is often said to be the most global sport in the world with Grand Prix taking place all over the globe in places as diverse as Bahrain, Canada, Azerbaijan, Brazil and Abu Dhabi, not to mention drivers who hail from such contrasting areas as Russia, Mexico, New Zealand and Denmark. However, did you know that the home of the sport is undoubtedly Great Britain?

How can that be, when the circuits and drivers are so diverse?!

Well, did you know that out of the 10 teams currently performing in F1, six of them have their headquarters right here in the UK?!

Currently Mercedes, McLaren, Williams, Red Bull, Force India and Renault call Britain home. Only Ferrari and Toro Rosso (Italy), Haas (USA) and Sauber (Switzerland) buck the trend.

Why is it though that a country with only one Grand Prix and none of the biggest car manufacturers involved in the sport is seen as the technological home of F1? The answer to this can be traced back to the roots of

the sport. Formula 1 did not come into existence until 1950, five years after the Second World War. At this time, Britain was seen as the perfect place to set up camp due to a large number of now unused airfields that could be used for testing, as well as an abundance of engineers, most with aeronautical experience all looking for something to do after the war was over. You may wonder why an aeroplane engineer would be so sought after by a team looking to design and build a race car but remember that a lot of the technology that goes into keeping a F1 car on the ground at high speed is just adapted and upside down plane technology used for keeping them in the air!

All of these factors attracted those who wanted to race with many of the old airfields being converted into race tracks. This in turn meant that suppliers and mechanics flocked to Britain, particularly the south east of England (where the majority of the teams are based) to get their fix and find employment in the vastly growing motorsport scene.

At first, it was not the teams but independent engineering firms that set up in the area designing and manufacturing cars and engines that they would then sell off to racing teams. One of the most famous of these firms was March Engineering, who provided World Championship winning engines. This was shortly followed by the likes of McLaren, Williams and Brabham setting up in the area and an industry was born.

There are also major logistical benefits to all of the teams being located so close to each other. Firstly, the transport links are excellent meaning equipment can be moved around the globe as required; Silverstone was very easy to get to for testing purposes and with a lot of teams close together, this gave many opportunities to the staff as they could move between teams if they wished without the need to relocate and uproot their families.

» OUT OF THE 10 TEAMS CURRENTLY PERFORMING IN F1, SIX OF THEM HAVE THEIR HEADQUARTERS RIGHT HERE IN THE UK.

AN ESTIMATED 80% OF THE WORLD'S HIGH PERFORMANCE SPECIALIST ENGINEERS LIVE IN WHAT HAS BEEN DUBBED FORMULA 1'S 'SILICON VALLEY'

By the late 1960s it was said that if you were serious about taking part in Formula 1, then you had to stay in the south-east of England and as late on as 2015, eight of the 10 teams competing were still based there. As always in F1, teams come and go and with advances in technology making it easier than ever to move and share information and goods, a few teams have bucked the trend and set-up operations away from the traditional hub. However, it could be argued that when you look at the teams that have, such as Toro Rosso and Haas, they have done so with limited success.

Of course, alongside the F1 teams comes the offshoot industries required such as transport, logistics, supplies, catering, administration staff and everything that goes into running a high performing company. With that in mind, it is now believed that there are approximately 3500 companies based in southern England that are directly linked to F1 or motorsport employing around 40,000 among them, with big manufacturers such as McLaren or Mercedes employing around 700 people each and even smaller F1 teams such as Force India around half of this. On top of this, an estimated 80% of the world's high performance specialist engineers live in what has been dubbed Formula 1's 'Silicon Valley'.

So it is easy to see why the UK is the home of the majority of teams with some surprising names on the list of teams based here; for example, when you hear the name Force India, would you think it was based right here in Great Britain?! The same goes for Mercedes, a manufacturer who is known for their German heritage – while their road cars are German designed and manufactured, the F1 team is another that calls Britain home. Renault, the most famous of French car manufacturers, are another.

With the level of expertise and history that exists in Great Britain this is not something that many see changing soon either. Taking the 2017 season as an example, 15 of the 20 races were won by a British designed and engineered machine with the only exception being Sebastian Vettel's five wins in his Italian Ferrari. It could be argued in fact that in the history of F1, only the famous Ferrari team have bucked the trend when it comes to being able to compete while not being UK based and they have a rich and varied history of their own.

So with six of the teams currently competing in Formula 1 all based within a few hours of each other right here in Great Britain, not to mention the current World Champion, Lewis Hamilton, and Constructors' Champion, Mercedes, all calling the UK home, then it is clear to see that the true home of F1 is most definitely Great Britain.

WORDSEARCH

Find the words in the grid. Words can go horizontally, vertically and diagonally in all eight directions.

O	L	T	F	N	A	I	D	N	I	E	C	R	O	F	G	W
D	T	L	N	J	L	F	Z	C	L	R	N	N	C	K	Q	T
R	R	U	M	E	R	C	E	D	E	S	T	K	K	Q	C	D
A	M	A	G	N	T	P	M	K	T	O	S	N	O	L	A	K
I	T	N	Z	D	E	M	Z	Z	T	D	B	L	H	J	T	W
C	B	E	N	Z	K	P	F	F	E	P	T	P	P	G	I	G
C	T	R	Q	J	P	T	P	N	V	Y	M	Q	R	L	G	K
I	B	O	T	T	A	S	O	A	D	N	F	N	L	K	G	M
R	O	X	Z	W	M	T	F	R	T	S	N	I	W	R	N	M
L	K	S	D	L	L	Y	E	E	T	S	A	T	E	E	M	A
V	Y	B	S	I	P	B	T	R	R	M	R	B	X	D	H	S
R	M	L	M	O	U	E	O	F	S	R	N	E	R	B	N	S
T	H	A	R	A	R	L	R	H	M	E	A	P	V	U	V	A
D	H	A	S	K	L	O	M	E	K	L	L	R	H	L	L	K
M	Y	M	A	Y	M	R	R	L	Z	N	J	Q	I	L	N	R
Z	L	K	G	S	K	T	U	O	W	M	C	L	A	R	E	N
X	Z	N	K	C	K	H	Z	G	T	J	T	V	R	X	F	T

Alonso

Bottas

Ferrari

ForceIndia

Haas

Hamilton

Hulkenberg

Massa

McLaren

Mercedes

Perez

RedBull

Renault

Ricciardo

Sauber

Stroll

ToroRosso

Verstappen

Vettel

Williams

ANSWERS ON
**PAGE
60-61**

CROSSWORD

ACROSS

1 Venue of the Hungarian Grand Prix (11)

3 Team name: Force _____ (5)

5 Lance, Williams driver for 2018 (6)

7 Jenson, last British driver to win a World Championship before Lewis Hamilton (6)

8 City that hosts the USA Grand Prix (6)

10 Brazilian three-time Championship Winner (6,5)

11 Famous part of Monaco circuit where drivers race round the harbour (3,6)

15 Team known as the 'Scuderia' (7)

17 Street circuit Grand Prix held in famous Asian city (9)

18 Kevin, Danish-born 2018 Haas driver (9)

19 2017 Constructors' Champion (7)

DOWN

2 Romain, Haas Ferrari driver (8)

4 Nationality of Daniel Ricciardo (10)

6 Venue for 2018 German Grand Prix (10)

9 Nico, German who retired after winning 2016 Championship (7)

12 Fernando, Spanish-born McLaren driver (6)

13 Venue of the final Grand Prix of 2018 season (3,5)

14 David, Scottish driver who raced in 246 Grand Prix between 1994 and 2008 (9)

15 Nationality of Ferrari's Kimi Raikkonen (7)

16 Sebastian, driver known as 'Il Botas' (6)

ANSWERS ON PAGE 60-61

MAX VERSTAPPEN

It is hard to believe that Max Verstappen did not reach his 21st birthday until the 2018 season given his performances and experience in the sport so far.

Son of former F1 driver, Jos Verstappen, and Kart Champion, Sophie Kumpen, it always seemed destined that Max would follow in their footsteps and take to the track, but the level of his success at such a young age must have come as a surprise to all. In saying that, there had been several pointers to the success that was to come, with Verstappen sweeping all before him in nearly every class he raced in as he progressed through his career, including karting and Formula 3.

Verstappen was just 17 years and 166 days old when he made his Grand Prix debut and still holds numerous records including Youngest Ever to Start a Grand Prix; Youngest to Lead a Grand Prix; Youngest to set the Fastest Lap in a Grand Prix; Youngest Points Scorer ever; Youngest Podium Finisher ever and Youngest Race Winner ever - that race win meaning he also became the first Dutchman ever to win a F1 race (although born in Belgium, Verstappen rides under the Dutch banner) – an impressive list!

Now with over 70 races to his name, many believe that with an injury free career and remaining in competitive cars that Verstappen could go on and outstrip a whole host of records in his career, not least multiple World Championships.

FACTFILE

DATE OF BIRTH:
30th September 1997

BORN: Hasselt, Belgium

BEST CHAMPIONSHIP FINISH: 5th, 2016

TEAM: Red Bull

DANIEL RICCIARDO

Another driver looking to take that next step and be crowned World Champion is Red Bull's Aussie racer Daniel Ricciardo.

Ricciardo is now a veteran on the grid having taken part in over 140 Grand Prix in his career and it seems he is only getting better with age. One of the most feared competitors on any racetrack, many feel it is just the lack of cutting edge from his Red Bull machine that has stopped him from reaching greater heights.

Born into a racing family, Ricciardo has said his earliest memories are of watching his father race around circuits in Western Australia, where he was born and raised. Joe Ricciardo, Daniel's father, was a keen amateur racer and collector of classic cars and this is where Daniel's love of racing materialised.

Starting as most do in karting at age nine before moving onto Formula Ford racing at 15, it

was immediately noticeable that Ricciardo had what it took to get to the top. Quick progressions through Formula Renault and Formula 3 would follow before the step to F1.

By this point, Ricciardo had been snapped up by the Red Bull Junior racing team and progressed through their ranks, also getting his first F1 drive with the now-defunct Hispania Racing Team. A move to Red Bull feeder team Toro Rosso would follow the next year before the move to Red Bull in 2014. This brought him his first ever Grand Prix victory in the same year at the Canadian Grand Prix.

While fortunes have fluctuated and there have been many changes at the Red Bull team in Ricciardo's five years there, he remained a constant in the team, carrying on the heritage of Australian drivers in his replacement of Mark Webber. However, with time running out

FACTFILE

DATE OF BIRTH:
1st July 1989

BORN: Perth, Australia

BEST CHAMPIONSHIP FINISH: 3rd 2014, 2016

TEAM: Renault

for a Championship tilt, and with the emergence of Max Verstappen looking likely to push Ricciardo to a secondary role, he has made the jump to Renault. Time will tell if this proves to push Ricciardo onto that top step of the podium.

MCLAREN TEAM

One of the most storied teams in the history of F1 is England-based McLaren. First appearing in F1 in 1966, McLaren has been ever-present since then and now the team is enjoying its fifth decade in the sport.

McLaren was founded by Bruce McLaren, a New Zealand born race car designer, driver, engineer and inventor who sadly died in a track crash aged just 32 when testing his latest car design. McLaren's name lives on though through the team's continued success in F1.

One of the most successful teams in the history of F1, McLaren have claimed eight Constructors' Championships over the years and their drivers have claimed 12 Drivers' Championships in their time, including the likes of Ayrton Senna, Mika Häkkinen and Lewis Hamilton.

The last few years have not been as kind to McLaren as they have slipped down the rankings but with their long history of success, it won't be long until they are back at the head of the podium.

CURRENT DRIVERS

FERNANDO ALONSO

DATE OF BIRTH: 29th July 1981
BORN: Oviedo, Spain
BEST CHAMPIONSHIP FINISH:
World Champion (2005, 2006)

One of four former World Champions currently still racing in F1 is Spaniard Alonso. He is now one of the most experienced men on the grid with over 300 Grand Prix starts to his name. Although his best days may now be behind him, Alonso is still universally popular and in a more competitive car, many still feel he would be challenging for titles once again.

STOFFEL VANDOORNE

DATE OF BIRTH: 26th March 1992
BORN: Kortrijk, Belgium
BEST CHAMPIONSHIP FINISH: 16th (2017)

The opposite end of the experience scale from Alonso is teammate Stoffel Vandoorne. 2018 was only his second full season in the sport. Vandoorne impressed with his steady performances improving as the season progressed and finishing the season in 16th position with three points finishes, including consecutive seventh place finishes in Singapore and Malaysia. The young Belgian will now be looking to improve on this as he gains more racing experience.

GREATEST RIVALRIES

With a history dating back to 1950 and a high octane culture, Formula 1 can lay claim to some of the greatest sporting rivalries the world has ever seen.

The very essence of F1 lies in each individual driver trying to be the best and with only one man being able to call himself World Champion come the end of the year, clashes and a dislike for anyone standing in their way is sure to form.

Yes, there are teams and team orders and every driver will tell you that they all want to help their teammates in the paddock, not just on the track, win a Constructors' Championship, but F1 drivers do not get to where they are without a singular focus – the focus to be the best and move anyone who gets in their way.

With that in mind, let's take a look back through history at some of the greatest rivalries the sport has ever seen and just how they shaped Formula 1 as we know it.

NIKI LAUDA VS. JAMES HUNT

With a rivalry so fierce a Hollywood film was made about it [*Rush* directed by Ron Howard], Lauda and Hunt had extremely contrasting personalities but both had that one goal in mind – to become World Champion.

Lauda was known as a reserved character, his focus solely on doing everything he could to get every extra ounce out of himself and his machine, pushing it to the very limit in search of glory. Hunt on the other hand was an outgoing type, known as a party boy; he was very rarely seen without a drink in one hand and a model on his other arm.

This contrast in personalities made for some big clashes on the track, none more so than in 1976. Lauda had won the Championship in 1975 and was leading comfortably the following year when a horrendous crash in the German Grand Prix left the Austrian fighting

for his life suffering from severe burns after his car caught fire. Remarkably, just two months after surgery to repair his lungs, Lauda was back in the car and chasing down back to back world titles having missed only two Grand Prix.

In his absence, Hunt had eaten into Lauda's lead but the Englishman still sat second in the Championship as they headed to Monza in Italy and rode a remarkable race to finish fourth; with Hunt having been relegated to the back of the grid for a fuel irregularity, the Englishman could not make up any ground.

The next race in Canada was to be a turning point as Hunt took the chequered flag with Lauda dropping out of the points due to a gearbox malfunction. It was game on for the Championship once again; Hunt would take victory in the next race in the USA also, meaning that it all came down to the last race of the season in Japan, which they entered into with Lauda leading by three points.

This race was to go down as one for the ages as torrential rain made the track almost un-raceable. In fact, Lauda and others pulled out after two laps citing the conditions as life threatening. This meant Hunt just required third place to clinch glory and he duly did, although not without drama as he was forced to pit with three laps to go, then pass two different drivers on the final two laps to secure the third place needed and the title.

After their experiences, Hunt and Lauda did become friends before Hunt's untimely passing, but to this day, the 1976 season remains one of the most famous in Formula 1 history.

NIGEL MANSELL VS. NELSON PIQUET

In a weird quirk of the sport, some of the greatest rivalries ever witnessed have come from drivers who race for the same team and this was certainly the case between Mansell and Piquet.

Mansell viewed himself as the main man at the Williams team when, in 1986, Piquet joined with one of his stipulations being that he would be the number one driver. This did not sit well with Mansell and his clashes with Piquet on and off the track are probably responsible for handing the title to McLaren's Alain Prost.

Before the invention of all the computer technology that teams now rely on, there was a big advantage to being in what was viewed as the 'number one' car; with this going to Piquet, Mansell was not happy. There were to be many instances where the rivalry came to a head, not least after the Hungarian Grand Prix where Mansell found out that his team had been working on a new part that improved aerodynamics. Piquet had been told about this and had used it to help him win the race while it had been kept a secret on purpose from Mansell.

This rivalry would continue into the next year, but this time there was no one to stand in the way as the teammates battled hard for the title. As in most great rivalries, the two had differing styles in how they went about their business. Piquet was the most methodical

doing hours upon hours of testing so that he knew his car was race ready and he built his Championship on consistency as, remarkably, Mansell actually won three more races than Piquet during the season but this was mixed in with non-point finishes.

Mansell was the more natural racer of the two; happy to use Piquet's set-up from practice and go out and race. This was to be his downfall as that inability to finish races would cost him the Championship as the Brazilian took his third World Title.

Off-track there was personal animosity also, with Mansell taking legal action against Piquet for comments about his wife. Piquet would move on from Williams after the 1987 season allowing Mansell to take on the much-craved mantle of number one driver and a title would come the Englishman's way in 1992.

ALAIN PROST VS. AYRTON SENNA

Perhaps the most famous of all Formula 1 rivalries came between

Senna in the late 80s. Again, this was a tale of two men who wanted to be number one in the same team.

1988 saw Senna join Prost at McLaren; a move which the at that time the two-time World Champion was not happy about, as he still viewed himself as the number one driver in the world despite having lost his title to Nelson Piquet the year before.

This relationship would only deteriorate when Senna pushed Prost almost into the pit wall at high-speed at the Portuguese Grand Prix. There were various other media spats, with Prost stating that he was frightened of driving with Senna as he was willing to do anything to win. Senna went on to win the title in 1988, but it was the next year where the rivalry really came to a head.

During the Grand Prix at Imola, Senna passed Prost after a restart in which Gerhard Berger's car had caught fire. Prost was furious, saying that the team and drivers had an agreement that they would not attempt to pass each other at this notoriously dangerous part of

This would not be the end of clashes as at the penultimate Grand Prix of the year they clashed again. Prost was leading the Championship with Senna needing to win the race to have any chance of lifting the title. In the closing laps, the two collided, with Prost believing this was intentional from Senna, the result being that Prost was forced to retire and Senna went on to win the race. However, after the race, the stewards determined that Senna had illegally rejoined the track and he was disqualified, handing the title to his teammate in the process.

The next year was to be even more controversial. By this point, Prost had decided he could not work with Senna anymore and had made the move to Ferrari. Once again, it was to be Japan and the second-to-last Grand Prix of the season that was to decide the Championship with Senna ahead by nine points. Senna gained the pole but was beaten to the first corner by the Frenchman. Senna then deliberately smashed into Prost's car forcing both of them out of the race and, at a time when you only got nine points for a win and with Senna holding the tiebreaker between the two, this meant the Championship was

2016 FORMULA 1 ETIHAD AIRWAYS ABU DHABI G

The rivalry would continue until Prost retired in 1993 when, remarkably, the two became friends; this being a true turn-up for the books as when they raced each other, they refused to mention each other by name, let alone shake hands or socialise together. Tragically, the friendship was cut short when Senna died in an on-track crash in 1994.

LEWIS HAMILTON VS. NICO ROSBERG

While many of the great rivalries of F1 took place in the 1980s and early 1990s, an era when car development was moving rapidly and some of the best drivers ever to grace the track raced, that is not to say that there are not equivalents in the modern day. One of these was the rivalry between Lewis Hamilton and Nico Rosberg, once again as teammates when they both raced with Mercedes.

One difference in this rivalry was that the two were in fact great friends from their teenage years before this turned to rivalry as both chased the world title they thought they deserved. Teammates from as early as 2000 in the Karting Championship, they were great friends often

seen sharing pizza and ice cream, kicking about a football and playing table tennis dreaming of being F1 teammates together.

The relationship would start to sour through their second year as teammates in 2014. Rosberg appeared to deliberately block Hamilton in qualifying at Monaco costing the Brit pole. More drama was to follow, most famously later that year at Spa when the two teammates collided, with Hamilton accusing Rosberg of doing this deliberately 'to prove a point'. This caused Hamilton to retire and forced Rosberg to replace his front wing, although he did recover to finish second. In the end, it did not have any bearing

on the Championship as Hamilton won comfortably by 67 points above his teammate.

The tension would not thaw though as once again the two battled for the title in 2015 – again the Englishman came out on top.

2016 would be Rosberg's turn to take the title before he remarkably retired from the sport but the animosity was there for all to see as the season progressed with on-track scuffles being matched with off-track verbal digs at each other's expense. Hamilton was of the belief that he was by far and away the best driver that year and only mechanical issues stopped him from claiming a third title in a row.

With Rosberg's retirement, no one will know if he would have been able to continue to best Hamilton, who regained his title in 2017, but there appears to be no reconciliation so far between the two.

With the way that F1 moves on, who is to say when and who will be the next great rivalry that captures the imagination of the fans. Who do you think it will be?!

THE PRANCING HORSE:
»FERRARI IN F1

When you think of the history of Formula 1, and all the drivers and constructors that have come and gone, there is one image that always sticks out in your head and that is the distinctive black prancing horse on the red Ferrari car. A founder member of the Championship back in 1950, Ferrari are the only team to have competed in every year of F1 and have an unprecedented level of success with 16 Constructors' Championships and 15 Drivers' Championships to their name in almost 70 years of racing innovation.

Founded by Enzo Ferrari, Scuderia Ferrari (to give the racing division of the manufacturer its full title), the racing team was set up in 1929. Remarkably, it was initially set up to race cars manufactured by another company, Alfa Romeo.

In 1938, Alfa Romeo decided to race under their own banner and this led to Ferrari starting to develop a race car of their own, although this was quickly halted by World War II, with the Ferrari factory being used for machine tool work. After the war was over, Ferrari went back to work on developing racing cars and, with the recruitment of several ex-employees from the Alfa Romeo days, they were ready to race again.

Ascari and Gonzalez at the British Grand Prix, 1953

Ascari at the Italian Grand Prix, 1959

Michael Schumacher, 1996

Ferrari's first Grand Prix was in Monaco in 1950 and the first ever Grand Prix victory came in the 1951 British Grand Prix, breaking the stranglehold that Alfa Romeo had on Formula 1 at the time. Alberto Ascari, Raymond Sommer and Gigi Villoresi were the first ever drivers to race in a Grand Prix for the team. It was to be another driver, José Froilán González, who was to be the hero of the day when he took that first victory at Silverstone.

This was to be the precursor of things to come as in 1952, Ferrari dominated the sport winning all bar one of the Grand Prix that year, with Ascari

becoming the first Ferrari World Champion, a feat he was to repeat the next year.

A lean couple of years would follow before the capture of Juan Manuel Fangio in 1956 propelled the team to another Championship.

The 60s were not a successful time as advances in technology coupled with the change in rules meant that only two Championships were gained in this time, these coming in 1961 and 1964. It must be said that it was only the reliability of the car, rather than the speed it

Enzo Ferrari

Ferrari with Alberto Ascari

Niki Lauda flies around Brands Hatch in his Ferrari 312 B3 at the qualifying race for the British Grand Prix, 1974

Schumacher at the Australian Grand Prix, 1997

possessed, that led to the later of these two victories!

This barren spell continued into the next decade and it would be 1975 before the team would taste victory in either the Constructors' or Drivers' Championship again. A period of success would follow with the team taking Constructors' titles in 1975, 1976, 1977, 1979, 1982 and 1983, alongside Drivers' glory in 1975 and 1977 for Niki Lauda and 1979 for Jody Scheckter.

Ferrari would then suffer its worst spell in the sport as it took a further 16 years before Constructors' glory was tasted again in 1999, with Drivers' gold eluding the Scuderia for 21 years after Scheckter's title, before Michael Schumacher claimed glory in 2000.

The second half of the 1980s was a particularly disappointing time for the team, compounded by the death of founder Enzo Ferrari in 1988. This did lead to one bright spot for the team though, as Gerhard

Berger and Michele Alboreto took first and second place at Ferrari's home track of Monza on an emotional day to remember the founder.

This lack of success continued into the 90s with even World Champions, Alain Prost and Nigel Mansell, brought in from other teams, failing to deliver the much sought after title.

Things were to take an upturn in the 1996 season when two-time reigning champion, Michael Schumacher, was brought in to partner Eddie Irvine in the cockpit, and with Schumacher's technical director and chief designer also coming from the Brawn racing team, better times were ahead!

The first few years of this new partnership were promising, although reliability issues stopped any real title challenges. Then, the

Schumacher celebrates winning the Italian Grand Prix, 1996

Sebastian Vettel celebrates victory on the podium during the 2018 British Grand Prix at Silverstone

Raikkonen in Ferrari SF7IH at the World Championship, Silverstone, 2018

NOTABLE DRIVERS

With 16 Constructors' Championships and 15 Drivers' Championships, the history of Ferrari is littered with names that stand tall against the all-time greats of the sport with the likes of Alberto Ascari, Juan Manuel Fangio, Niki Lauda, Michael Schumacher, and most recently Kimi Räikkönen, all standing atop the podium at the end of the season for the Scuderia.

Schumacher is the most famous of these and also the most successful for the team. The German won five consecutive Drivers' Championships between 2000 and 2004, with the team also taking the Constructors' Championship in all of these years. Schumacher holds the record for Most Race Wins for Ferrari with 72 in total, a remarkable 57 ahead of closest rival Lauda who has 15.

There have also been numerous other World Champions who have raced in the famous red of Ferrari without tasting title glory of their own, including Fernando Alonso, Sebastian Vettel, Gilles Villeneuve, Alain Prost, and Nigel Mansell. The list of riders to have raced for the team really is a who's who of F1 Greats.

So, it has now been at least a 10 year wait since either of these titles and a lack of success is not something anyone is accustomed to at Ferrari. With an improved performance in the last season or two, it may not be longuntil we see the famous red back atop the podium once more.

1999 season looked to be the one that would see a Ferrari driver back atop the podium again, only for Schumacher to break his leg whilst leading the Championship, although the team did take the Constructors' Championship.

This was only to delay Ferrari and Schumacher's domination of the sport which would start in earnest in 2000. Five straight individual titles were to come the German's way with the Constructors' Championship added in each of those years also.

Schumacher would announce his retirement as of the end of the 2006 season and his reign of dominance was over. Ferrari chose Fin, Kimi Räikkönen, to take over from Schumacher and 'The Iceman' as he is nicknamed duly won a world title in his first year with the team. The following year, 2008, was the last time the Prancing Horse secured the Constructors' Title.

RECORDS

With a history as gloried as that of Ferrari, it is no surprise that the team holds a vast majority of the All-Time records in Formula 1, including:

Most Constructors' Championships – 16

Most Drivers' Championships – 15

Most Grand Prix Participated – 963

Most Wins – 233

Most Podium Finishes – 742

Most 1-2 Finishes – 83

Most Pole Positions – 218

RENAULT TEAM

French manufacturer, Renault, have been a common, if not consistent, name in F1 over the years since it was first seen on the grid back in 1986. The current incarnation returned to the grid in 2016, taking over from the Lotus team and, despite being a famous French name, the F1 team is actually based in Britain. This was a return to the sport after its successful spell between 2002 and 2011.

Still looking to get back to the title winning ways of the past, Renault has improved year-on-year since its return as their self-manufactured engine gets better all the time. Time will tell whether this will be enough to get them back to their former glory as twice Constructors' Champion in 2005 and 2006, and Fernando Alonso raced to back to back Drivers' Championships. The last few years have not been as kind, however with the pedigree and technology that lies behind the Renault team, success can't be far away.

»» CURRENT DRIVERS

NICO HÜLKENBERG

DATE OF BIRTH: 19th August 1987
BORN: Emmerich am Rhein, Germany
BEST CHAMPIONSHIP FINISH: 9th (2014, 2016)

With an experienced and steady hand, Nico Hülkenberg has been a stalwart of the F1 grid since 2010, despite a relative lack of success. The best race finish the German has managed in his career is fourth, but with his known work rate and team ethos, Hülkenberg is a popular man in the sport and this as much as his results keep him on the grid.

CARLOS SAINZ JR

DATE OF BIRTH: 1st September 1994
BORN: Madrid, Spain
BEST CHAMPIONSHIP FINISH: 9th (2017)

A famous name in motorsport is Carlos Sainz, Sainz Jr being the son of a former two-time World Rally Champion. Only in his early twenties, Sainz is making great strides in the sport having raced to his best ever position in 2017. Having being developed through the Red Bull Junior Team, Sainz certainly has the pedigree to get to the top although with no podium places to his name entering the 2018 season, an upturn in performance may be required if he is to go down as a driver of as high calibre as his dad.

HAAS TEAM

A relatively unknown name in F1 circles in 2016 when they joined the grid, American outfit, Haas, have made many sit up and take notice with their performances so far.

Although new to F1, Haas is not a new name to motorsport with a successful NASCAR team winning multiple championships in that discipline over the years. Founded by businessman Bill Haas, they are the first fully USA based team to take part in F1 in over 30 years. With little pedigree in the sport, Haas have taken many by surprise as they recorded eighth place finishes in the Championship in both 2016 and 2017, the former being the best debut by a team in many years.

This success may well be built on the fact that despite being an all American team, the majority of their technology comes from Ferrari. A long term deal is in place for engines, transmission and various other parts. If the Haas team can get the best out of this equipment, then a steady move up the standings appears to be in order.

▶▶ CURRENT DRIVERS

KEVIN MAGNUSSEN

DATE OF BIRTH: 5th October 1992
BORN: Roskilde, Denmark
BEST CHAMPIONSHIP FINISH: 11th (2014)

An experienced driver who has spent time in and out of F1 since 2014, unfortunately Magnussen has possibly never quite hit the heights that many expected when he made his F1 debut. This was magnified with the Dane racing to a second place finish in his first-ever Grand Prix, a result that remarkably is still his best-ever race finish.

Magnussen has shown flashes of that winning ability since, so hopefully his best result is yet to come.

ROMAIN GROSJEAN

DATE OF BIRTH: 17th April 1986
BORN: Geneva, Switzerland
BEST CHAMPIONSHIP FINISH: 7th (2013)

Another driver who has tasted podium success but never made it to the top step is Frenchman Romain Grosjean. Grosjean, who chooses to race under the French flag despite being born in Switzerland, has had a long and varied career having appeared in more than 120 Grand Prix. Known for being a good team man, Grosjean is also no slouch on the track with a seventh place finish his overall career best. It remains to be seen whether his best days are behind him as he heads into his thirties, but if the Haas car keeps improving, there could be one last hurrah.

STEP INTO F1

There is a fairly well worn path to hit F1 stardom, with most drivers starting out at a very young age (some as young as four) in the karting scene.

Any potential will lead to moving into single seater racing in the likes of Formula Renault, moving up through the ranks of the various Formulas of single seater racing before finding themselves in Formula 2, F1's support class which travels the world with the main tour acting as pre-F1 entertainment on race weekends.

Normally, by the time a driver gets to F2 they will have been heavily scouted by F1 teams and many will already be in driver training programmes with the likes of McLaren, Ferrari or Red Bull. Just who are these drivers that may be the next to make the step up into F1?!

GEORGE RUSSELL

20 year old Brit, George Russell, is really making a name for himself on the F2 scene, with many tipping him to be the next British World Champion.

2018 was his debut year at that level, but he has shown plenty of poise so far with the rookie leading the Championship halfway through the season. These types of performance are no surprise though given that he is already a Formula 3 World Champion and is the Mercedes reserve driver for the 2018 season. Russell was born in King's Lynn in the south-east of England, starting karting at eight years old. Having quickly progressed through the levels of karting, it was onto single seater racing and success came quickly at every level. This led to Russell being snapped up as part of the Mercedes driver training

program and, while having not competed in a Grand Prix as of yet, Russell is not far away having completed testing sessions for the likes of Force India alongside his parent outfit. Should this type of progression continue, then it is expected that Russell will be a permanent fixture on the grid sooner rather than later.

LANDO NORRIS

Another young Brit looking to emulate the likes of Lewis Hamilton is Bristol born 19 year old Lando Norris. Norris came

to racing from a slightly different background being that his family has no real racing pedigree. In his favour though was the fact that his father, Adam Norris, is a famous businessman in the UK with an estimated wealth of over £200 million. This meant that once Lando had shown the promise that would lead to him becoming World Karting Champion at only 14, the financial backing was there for Norris to live out his dream of becoming a F1 great. That is not to say that Norris is not supremely talented, his results so far mark him as good a prospect as has been seen for many a year. With championships galore at all levels, it would not be long before Norris was tied in to a F1 team and that team would be McLaren. Norris is part of their driver training programme and also the official test and reserve driver team for the 2018 season for McLaren. You should remember his name as no doubt Norris will be gracing the biggest stage of them all in a short space of time.

ARTEM MARKELOV

Born in 1994, Artem Markelov may not be quite as young as some of his rivals for the next available seats in F1, but with that also comes the advantage of an increased level of experience over them. Born in Moscow, Artem would be only the fourth ever Russian to make it to the F1 grid but, with Daniil Kvyat and Sergey Sirotkin having done so in recent years, the tide is turning for former eastern bloc drivers to make their mark. Markelov has been snapped up by Renault to be their chief development and test driver

for the 2018 season, this coming on the back of a second place finish in the 2017 F2 Championship. If he continues to progress and impress as he has done so far, then he will not be far away from a full time slot in the main series itself.

ALEXANDER ALBON

Although born in London, 22 year old Alexander Albon races under the flag of Thailand, meaning if he was to reach F1 in his career, he would be the first ever Thai driver to do so. Albon comes from racing pedigree with his father, Nigel Albon, a former British Touring Car racer. Like his contemporaries, karting was the first port of call for Albon starting at age eight and winning the title at all age groups

on the way through the ranks. Successful seasons in Formula Renault and the GP3 series were to follow. Albon was then snapped up as part of the Red Bull Junior Team and made the move to F2 to start the 2017 season. It was a little of an up-and-down debut season for Albon at that level with a mixture of great performances mixed in with some disappointing ones, the outcome being a 10th place finish overall. Albon appears to have made strides though and is making his experience count as he improved his performance into 2018 sitting in fourth at the halfway stage of the Championship. This is the kind of thing that F1 teams take notice of and if this level of improvement continues, Albon is another you can expect to see in the cockpit of a F1 car before very long.

So, there you have it – a list of names to keep an eye out for in the future. Who knows, you may just have read about the next great F1 Champion or, at the very least, you will now have some information to amaze your friends and family with when you next watch a Grand Prix and see one of these young drivers make their track debut!

Kimi Räikkönen leads the race during the German Grand Prix, July 2018.

FORCE INDIA TEAM

Now entering over a decade in the sport, the Force India team are renowned for their ability to punch above their weight and outperform expectations. Known for having largely young and exciting drivers who are progressing in the sport, this recipe has led to some fantastic results.

Another team that is based in Britain, this time at Silverstone, Force India's name derives from its Indian owner Vijay Mallya. The team itself has a storied F1 history having been known under different names. Prior to Mallya's purchase, the team raced under the Spyker brand and prior to that, was known as Jordan Grand Prix after its then owner and now TV commentator, Eddie Jordan.

While not able to quite replicate the success that Jordan once had when it recorded a high of third in the Constructors' Championship, the team continues to make strides with fourth place finishes in both 2016 and 2017 and it could be that the next step is not too far away.

►► CURRENT DRIVERS

SERGIO PÉREZ

DATE OF BIRTH: 26th January 1990
BORN: Guadalajara, Mexico
BEST CHAMPIONSHIP FINISH: 7th (2016, 2017)

One of the most popular sportsmen in his native Mexico, Sergio Pérez is close to becoming a global superstar. It may be that a race win or two is all that is standing in his way from that universal acclaim. A veteran of over 150 Grand Prix, Pérez has been close to the top but two second place finishes remain his best. This has not dampened the enthusiasm for his performances in his homeland, where he is beloved due to his pride in being Mexican and also his charity work, particularly with children. If Pérez can take the leap up to race winner, then there could be no stopping the charismatic racer.

ESTEBAN OCON

DATE OF BIRTH: 17th September 1996
BORN: Évreux, France
BEST CHAMPIONSHIP FINISH: 8th (2017)

A consistent if not spectacular performer, French youngster, Esteban Ocon, is making a name for himself as one to watch for the future. Having improved every year in his short F1 career, Ocon made people sit up and take notice as he recorded 18 point finishes from 20 races in 2017. If these results can progress into podiums and race wins, then a Championship may lie in his future.

TORO ROSSO TEAM

Formed in 2006, Toro Rosso's main aim is to provide a proving ground for drivers coming through the Red Bull Junior team to see if these drivers are then ready to take the next step up to the main Red Bull team.

That being said though, Toro Rosso are not just on the grid to make up the numbers and have acquitted themselves well with some surprisingly good results over the years, not least a race win for Sebastian Vettel who would then go on to win four World Titles with the Red Bull Team.

One of the few teams not based in the UK, Toro Rosso are headquartered in Italy (Toro Rosso translates as Red Bull in Italian) and utilise a Honda engine. The register of drivers who have been given their chance at Toro Rosso is very impressive, with the likes of Sebastian Vettel, Daniel Ricciardo, Daniil Kvyat, Carlos Sainz Jr and Max Verstappen all having made the step on to other F1 teams, normally the full Red Bull team.

This philosophy of promoting drivers at a young age is obviously working and who knows when the team will next unearth another future World Champion.

CURRENT DRIVERS

PIERRE GASLY

DATE OF BIRTH: 7th February 1996
BORN: Rouen, France
BEST CHAMPIONSHIP FINISH: 21st (2017)

There appears to be an abundance of young French talent coming through the F1 ranks just now and Pierre Gasly is another of these.

Given his debut towards the end of the 2017 season, Gasly did enough to maintain his position despite not managing to trouble the scorers.

A better year will be required if the former Karting Champion is to maintain his F1 spot.

BRENDON HARTLEY

DATE OF BIRTH: 10th November 1989
BORN: Palmerston North, New Zealand
BEST CHAMPIONSHIP FINISH: 23rd (2017)

On the other end of the age scale, and going against the normal Toro Rosso mandate of developing younger drivers, is Brendon Hartley. The New Zealand born racer will not look to give up his spot without a fight though having battled back to the F1 scene after being dropped by the Red Bull training programme seven years before Toro Rosso brought him back to the grid halfway through the 2017 season. Despite a fruitless few races points wise, Hartley was deemed to have done enough to warrant a second chance; whether a third chance will be offered if the points do not come is unsure.

WILLIAMS TEAM

Another of the most famous teams in the history of F1 comes in the form of Williams Racing. Having been part of F1 since all the way back in 1978, there aren't many teams who can lay claim to the level of success that has been brought to the team, and its owner and Team Chief Sir Frank Williams, over the last 40 years.

With nine Constructors' Championships to their name alongside seven Drivers' Championships, 114 Grand Prix victories and 128 pole positions, only Ferrari and McLaren can claim to have the same level of success over a sustained period of time. With a history of success like that, it is no surprise that some of the sport's greatest ever drivers have sat behind the wheel of a Williams car at one point or another including Keke Rosberg, Nigel Mansell, Damon Hill, Alain Prost, Nelson Piquet and Ayrton Senna.

Times have been tough in recent years for Williams though as they have not been able to remain competitive with their rivals and find themselves in an unusual position towards the back of the grid in most Grand Prix. With their history and expertise at their disposal, it would be foolish to think this will be a long-term slide though.

CURRENT DRIVERS

SERGEY SIROTKIN

DATE OF BIRTH: 27th August 1995
BORN: Moscow, Russia
BEST CHAMPIONSHIP FINISH: N/A (debut season)

A rookie in the 2018 season, Sergey Sirotkin remarkably became only the third ever Russian to have a permanent slot in a F1 team. While a newcomer to F1, Sirotkin does have some impressive results to his name in both the F2 and Le Mans racing series, and at only 22 years old when the season started, was viewed as an exciting prospect. Whether he can make the breakthrough and go further than any of his countrymen have remains to be seen but the signs are positive early in his career.

LANCE STROLL

DATE OF BIRTH: 29th October 1998
BORN: Montreal, Canada
BEST CHAMPIONSHIP FINISH: 12th (2017)

Another of a crop of exciting youngsters that look ready to take over the mantle form the likes of Lewis Hamilton and Sebastian Vettel in the not too distant future is Canadian, Lance Stroll. Despite being only 19 at the start of the 2018 season, Stroll was already a veteran of a full season where he made the podium in Azerbaijan – an almost unbelievable achievement for a young driver. With flashes of potential and time to learn, Stroll is expected to be a fixture on the grid for years to come.

SAUBER TEAM

Another team with a varied if, in this case, largely unsuccessful F1 history is Swiss outfit Sauber, or Alfa Romeo Sauber F1 Team to give them their full title.

A mainstay in the paddock since 1993, Sauber have done well to maintain competitiveness throughout all the changes that the sport has seen in those 25 years, but it has to be said with only one Grand Prix win and 27 podium finishes in that time, they will not go down as one of the more successful of teams in the modern era. This sole Grand Prix victory also came when the team raced as the BMW team known as Sauber BMW at the time and with the support of BMW behind it.

That is not down to a lack of trying though and founder, Peter Sauber, has always strived for the best he can and asks for no less from the rest of his team. Many drivers have used Sauber as a stepping stone before moving onto greatness elsewhere, not least seven-time World Champion Michael Schumacher.

The last few years have been particularly unkind to Sauber with the team not able to raise above eighth in the Constructors' standings at season end in any year since 2013. It is hoped the new partnership with Alfa Romeo, which came into force in 2018, will help improve fortunes though and early signs are positive for this.

CURRENT DRIVERS

CHARLES LECLERC

DATE OF BIRTH: 16th October 1997
BORN: Monte Carlo, Monaco
BEST CHAMPIONSHIP FINISH: N/A (debut season)

One of only two newcomers to F1 in 2018 is Monaco-born Charles Leclerc. Another in an impressive crop of youngsters that are rising the ranks just now, Leclerc was one of the youngest drivers in the grid during the 2018 season, at only 20 years old. That is not to say that Leclerc is not an experienced racer though having been F2 champion in 2017, as well as a member of the Ferrari test team alongside further test outings for Haas and Sauber in 2017. These test runs for Sauber must have made an impression as the new driver was invited to join the team with a full drive for 2018.

MARCUS ERICSSON

DATE OF BIRTH: 2nd September 1990
BORN: Kumla, Sweden
BEST CHAMPIONSHIP FINISH: 18th (2015)

As a veteran of over 80 Grand Prix, many may wonder if time is running out for Sweden's Marcus Ericsson. A prolific Champion coming up through the ranks, the top flight appears to have been a step too far with a career best Championship Finish of 18th. As the last points he scored in that best season of 2015 were the last time he troubled the scorers at all, there cannot be too many chances left for Ericsson.

Valtteri Bottas at the British Grand Prix, July 2018.

FACTS AND STATS

MOST WORLD CHAMPIONSHIPS:
Michael Schumacher – 7

YOUNGEST WORLD CHAMPION:
Sebastian Vettel – won in 2010 at 23 years and 135 days old

OLDEST WORLD CHAMPION:
Juan Manuel Fangio – won in 1957 at 46 years and 41 days old

MOST RACE WINS:
Michael Schumacher – 91 wins

PERCENTAGE OF RACES WON:
Juan Manuel Fangio won 24 of 52 races = 46.15% win rate

MOST WINS IN A SEASON:
Michael Schumacher – 13 wins

MOST CONSECUTIVE WINS:
Sebastian Vettel – 9 wins

YOUNGEST WINNER:
Max Verstappen – 18 years and 228 days old

OLDEST WINNER:
Luigi Fagioli – 53 years and 22 days old

MOST WINS IN THE SAME GRAND PRIX:
Michael Schumacher – 8 wins in the French Grand Prix

MOST CHAMPIONSHIP POINTS IN A SEASON:
Sebastian Vettel – 397 points in the 2013 season

YOUNGEST DRIVER TO SCORE A POINT:
Max Verstappen – 17 years and 180 days in the 2015 Malaysian Grand Prix

OLDEST DRIVER TO SCORE POINTS:
Phillippe Étancelin – 53 years and 249 days in the 1950 Italian Grand Prix

MOST CONSTRUCTORS' CHAMPIONSHIPS:
Ferrari – 16

MOST CONSTRUCTORS' WINS:
Ferrari – 233

MOST CONSTRUCTORS' POLE POSITIONS:
Ferrari – 218

MOST CONSTRUCTORS' PODIUMS:
Ferrari – 742

MOST RACES EVER:
Rubens Barrichello – 326 Races

YOUNGEST DRIVER TO START A RACE:
Max Verstappen – 17 years and 166 days old

OLDEST DRIVER TO START A RACE:
Louis Chiron – 55 years and 292 days old

MOST POLE POSITIONS:
Lewis Hamilton – 77 poles

MOST POLE POSITIONS IN A SEASON:
Sebastian Vettel – 15 poles

PODIUM FINISHES:
Michael Schumacher – 155 podiums

MOST PODIUMS IN A SEASON:
Michael Schumacher – 17 podiums

MOST CONSECUTIVE PODIUM FINISHES:
Michael Schumacher – 19 podiums

MOST POINT FINISHES:
Michael Schumacher – 221 points finishes

DRIVERS' CHAMPIONSHIP WINNERS

YEAR	NATIONALITY	NAME	CONSTRUCTOR	YEAR	NATIONALITY	NAME	CONSTRUCTOR
1950		Giuseppe Farina	Alfa Romeo	1983		Nelson Piquet	Brabham
1951		Juan Manuel Fangio	Alfa Romeo	1984		Niki Lauda	McLaren
1952		Alberto Ascari	Ferrari	1985		Alain Prost	McLaren
1953		Alberto Ascari	Ferrari	1986		Alain Prost	McLaren
1954		Juan Manuel Fangio	Maserati Mercedes	1987		Nelson Piquet	Williams
1955		Juan Manuel Fangio	Mercedes	1988		Ayrton Senna	McLaren
1956		Juan Manuel Fangio	Ferrari	1990		Ayrton Senna	McLaren
1957		Juan Manuel Fangio	Maserati	1991		Ayrton Senna	McLaren
1958		Mike Hawthorn	Ferrari	1992		Nigel Mansell	Williams
1959		Jack Brabham	Cooper	1993		Alain Prost	Williams
1960		Jack Brabham	Cooper	1994		Michael Schumacher	Benetton
1961		Phil Hill	Ferrari	1995		Michael Schumacher	Benetton
1962		Graham Hill	BRM	1996		Damon Hill	Williams
1963		Jim Clark	Lotus	1997		Jacques Villeneuve	Williams
1964		John Surtees	Ferrari	1998		Mika Häkkinen	McLaren
1965		Jim Clark	Lotus	1999		Mika Häkkinen	McLaren
1966		Jack Brabham	Brabham	2000		Michael Schumacher	Ferrari
1967		Denny Hulme	Brabham	2001		Michael Schumacher	Ferrari
1968		Graham Hill	Lotus	2002		Michael Schumacher	Ferrari
1969		Jackie Stewart	Matra	2003		Michael Schumacher	Ferrari
1970		Jochen Rindt	Lotus	2004		Michael Schumacher	Ferrari
1971		Jackie Stewart	Tyrrell	2005		Fernando Alonso	Renault
1972		Emerson Fittipaldi	Lotus	2006		Fernando Alonso	Renault
1973		Jackie Stewart	Tyrrell	2007		Kimi Räikkönen	Ferrari
1974		Emerson Fittipaldi	McLaren	2008		Lewis Hamilton	McLaren
1975		Niki Lauda	Ferrari	2009		Jenson Button	Brawn
1976		James Hunt	McLaren	2010		Sebastian Vettel	Red Bull
1977		Niki Lauda	Ferrari	2011		Sebastian Vettel	Red Bull
1978		Mario Andretti	Lotus	2012		Sebastian Vettel	Red Bull
1979		Jody Scheckter	Ferrari	2013		Sebastian Vettel	Red Bull
1980		Alan Jones	Williams	2014		Lewis Hamilton	Mercedes
1981		Nelson Piquet	Brabham	2015		Lewis Hamilton	Mercedes
1982		Keke Rosberg	Williams	2016		Nico Rosberg	Mercedes
				2017		Lewis Hamilton	Mercedes

CONSTRUCTORS' CHAMPIONSHIP WINNERS

YEAR	CONSTRUCTOR	DRIVERS
1958	Vanwall	Stirling Moss, Tony Brooks
1959	Cooper	Jack Brabham, Stirling Moss, Bruce McLaren
1960	Cooper	Jack Brabham, Bruce McLaren
1961	Ferrari	Phil Hill, Wolfgang von Trips
1962	BRM	Graham Hill
1963	Lotus	Jim Clark
1964	Ferrari	John Surtees, Lorenzo Bandini
1965	Lotus	Jim Clark
1966	Brabham	Jack Brabham
1967	Brabham	Denny Hulme, Jack Brabham
1968	Lotus	Graham Hill, Jo Siffert, Jim Clark, Jackie Oliver
1969	Matra	Jackie Stewart, Jean-Pierre Beltoise
1970	Lotus	Jochen Rindt, Emerson Fittipaldi, Graham Hill, John Miles
1971	Tyrrell	Jackie Stewart, François Cevert
1972	Lotus	Emerson Fittipaldi
1973	Lotus	Emerson Fittipaldi, Ronnie Peterson
1974	McLaren	Emerson Fittipaldi, Denny Hulme, Mike Hailwood, David Hobbs, Jochen Mass
1975	Ferrari	Clay Regazzoni, Niki Lauda
1976	Ferrari	Niki Lauda, Clay Regazzoni
1977	Ferrari	Niki Lauda, Carlos Reutemann
1978	Lotus	Mario Andretti, Ronnie Peterson
1979	Ferrari	Jody Scheckter, Gilles Villeneuve
1980	Williams	Alan Jones, Carlos Reutemann
1981	Williams	Alan Jones, Carlos Reutemann
1982	Ferrari	Gilles Villeneuve, Didier Pironi, Patrick Tambay, Mario Andretti
1983	Ferrari	Patrick Tambay, René Arnoux
1984	McLaren	Alain Prost, Niki Lauda
1985	McLaren	Niki Lauda, Alain Prost, John Watson
1986	Williams	Nigel Mansell, Nelson Piquet
1987	Williams	Nigel Mansell, Nelson Piquet, Riccardo Patrese
1988	McLaren	Alain Prost, Ayrton Senna

YEAR	CONSTRUCTOR	DRIVERS
1989	McLaren	Ayrton Senna, Alain Prost
1990	McLaren	Ayrton Senna, Gerhard Berger
1991	McLaren	Ayrton Senna, Gerhard Berger
1992	Williams	Nigel Mansell, Riccardo Patrese
1993	Williams	Damon Hill, Alain Prost
1994	Williams	Damon Hill, Ayrton Senna, David Coulthard, Nigel Mansell
1995	Benetton	Michael Schumacher, Johnny Herbert
1996	Williams	Damon Hill, Jacques Villeneuve
1997	Williams	Jacques Villeneuve, Heinz-Harald Frentzen
1998	McLaren	David Coulthard, Mika Häkkinen
1999	Ferrari	Michael Schumacher, Eddie Irvine, Mika Salo
2000	Ferrari	Michael Schumacher, Rubens Barrichello
2001	Ferrari	Michael Schumacher, Rubens Barrichello
2002	Ferrari	Michael Schumacher, Rubens Barrichello
2003	Ferrari	Michael Schumacher, Rubens Barrichello
2004	Ferrari	Michael Schumacher, Rubens Barrichello
2005	Renault	Fernando Alonso, Giancarlo Fisichella
2006	Renault	Fernando Alonso, Giancarlo Fisichella
2007	Ferrari	Felipe Massa, Kimi Räikkönen
2008	Ferrari	Kimi Räikkönen, Felipe Massa
2009	Brawn	Jenson Button, Rubens Barrichello
2010	Red Bull	Sebastian Vettel, Mark Webber
2011	Red Bull	Sebastian Vettel, Mark Webber
2012	Red Bull	Sebastian Vettel, Mark Webber
2013	Red Bull	Sebastian Vettel, Mark Webber
2014	Mercedes	Nico Rosberg, Lewis Hamilton
2015	Mercedes	Nico Rosberg, Lewis Hamilton
2016	Mercedes	Nico Rosberg, Lewis Hamilton
2017	Mercedes	Nico Rosberg, Lewis Hamilton

PUZZLE ANSWERS

P8-9: FACE IN THE CROWD

P33: WORDSEARCH

O	L	T	F	N	A	I	D	N	I	E	C	R	O	F	G	W
D	T	L	N	J	L	F	Z	C	L	R	N	N	C	K	Q	T
R	R	U	M	E	R	C	E	D	E	S	T	K	K	Q	C	D
A	M	A	G	N	T	P	M	K	T	O	S	N	O	L	A	K
I	T	N	Z	R	E	M	Z	Z	T	D	B	L	H	J	T	W
C	B	E	N	K	P	F	F	E	P	P	P	G	I	G		
C	T	R	Q	J	P	T	P	N	V	Y	Q	R	L	G	K	
I	B	O	T	T	A	S	O	A	D	N	F	N	L	K	G	M
R	O	X	Z	W	M	T	F	R	T	S	N	I	W	R	N	M
L	K	S	D	L	L	Y	E	E	T	S	A	T	E	E	M	A
V	Y	B	S	I	P	B	T	R	R	M	R	B	X	D	H	S
R	M	L	M	O	I	E	S	R	N	E	R	B	N	S		
T	H	A	R	A	R	L	R	H	M	E	A	P	V	U	V	A
D	H	A	S	K	L	O	M	E	K	L	L	R	H	L	L	K
M	Y	M	A	Y	M	R	L	Z	N	J	Q	I	L	N	R	
Z	L	K	G	S	K	T	U	O	W	M	C	L	A	R	E	N
X	Z	N	K	C	K	H	Z	G	T	J	T	V	R	X	F	T

P34: CROSSWORD

HUNGARORING
INDIA
STROLL
BUTTON AUSTIN
AYRTONSENNA
THEMARINA
COULTHARD
FERRARI
SINGAPORE
MAGNUSSEN
MCLAREN

60

1. Michael Schumacher
2. 46
3. 5
4. Silverstone
5. 10
6. French
7. McLaren and Mercedes
8. Fernando Alonso, Stoffel Vandoorne
9. 4
10. Monza
11. 37
12. Ferrari
13. 16
14. Charles Leclerc and Sergey Sirotkin
15. Australian Grand Prix
16. Lewis Hamilton, Sebastian Vettel, Fernando Alonso and Kimi Räikkönen
17. New Zealand
18. 10
19. 1950
20. Sebastian Vettel, Michael Schumacher
21. 13
22. 2
23. Alberto Ascari, Paul Hawkins
24. 6
25. Danish
26. 9
27. 2005, 2006
28. Montreal
29. Ayrton Senna
30. 6
31. Sergio Pérez, Esteban Ocon
32. 2
33. Williams
34. Benetton, Ferrari
35. Rubens Barrichello
36. 2
37. Graham and Damon Hill, Keke and Nico Rosberg
38. 6
39. Stirling Moss, 16
40. Valtteri Bottas, 231.48 miles per hour